Success Is a Feeling

ANOTHER WAY TO SEE LIFE

This book is a map for anything you want.
All will make sense as you read on.

ALEX GAGEANU

Table of Contents

> "If you want to find the secrets of the universe think in terms of energy, frequency and vibration"

Nikola Tesla

Introduction

After years of research and experimentation, I ultimately concluded that, in truth, life is quite simple. And you are about to find out why.

Life is not inherently complicated; we are the ones who make it so. We let our minds run wild on a perpetual rollercoaster of worry, stress, and fear - especially fear - about anything and everything. We don't realise that we simply *have* a mind, - we are not our mind. Because of this, we never feel safe enough to be truly content, and we constantly seek greater and greater detail in order to take control of our lives. We feel the need to understand everything around us and acquire all possible knowledge to ultimately find a place of rest. It's funny if you think about it. We spend all our lives getting more and more knowledge from *outside* of us, without realizing the knowledge we have *inside* of us. We don't stop and look inside to discover ourselves, who we really are and how all this actually works.

The one thing you must always remember is that you are ENERGY. You are pure energy that vibrates. All of us, and everything around us, are made from the same thing; everything is connected to everything else. It is a fact of quantum theory that not only do particles consist of energy, but so does the space between them. This is the connection that binds us all. Everything that exists is connected because it is made of the same thing.

Everything is ONE energy! Now, if this concept is new to you and you feel that you need the details and fine print, I encourage you to look them up. Mountains of information and tests about molecules, atoms, vibration, energy, matter, the mind-body connection and so on exist, covering just about everything you can imagine on the subject. I could write about all of the incredible discoveries of man, from the beginning of recorded history to the present, and all the facts and theories to support them, in detail. This would create an impressive, literary work of art packed with details that you may never need, and that would doubtlessly complicate things. However, I've written this book to be simple, informative and thought-provoking for you, without the complications. As you read on, I ask that you consider not the size of this book, but rather its content.

For the sake of simplicity, I'm going to present the information here as straightforwardly as possible. Let's get to it!

If you put your hand under a microscope, you will notice that there is more space than solid matter. You can try this with anything else you want from this physical world, and you will discover the same thing. The reason why you see and feel your hand as solid is that your cells vibrate at a high frequency, making what they form *appear* solid when, in fact, they are not. You are *energy*, living in an ocean of energy, which vibrates constantly on different levels. When we say that our favorite people or places resonate with us, we may mean something more than a figure of speech. At the core level, you are energy, the same as everything else, and are therefore a part of everything.

Somewhere along the way, you started identifying yourself with your mind and, in the process, you forgot to *feel*. Try for a second to imagine yourself as having an energy tube, a channel if you will, that runs up your spine in constant communication with your mind, and everything else around you. Along that journey, you started blocking the tube with fear, worries, stress, regrets, unhappiness and so on. The list is long. Let's think of these negative feelings as little bits of mud, clogging your tube of energy. With all of this mud in the way, energy struggles to get through, so your mind fails to receive the information from the source.

In other words, it is left without instruction. Without proper guidance, your mind starts to worry, stress and create its own definitions of right and wrong. It is searching desperately for answers. At the same time, it is bombarded from all directions with threats, information, and rapid changes in situations from the outside world. All of this can get overwhelmingly complicated, and suck the fun out of life. You need to make it simpler. You need to lighten up. For that to happen, you must leave the world alone for a bit, and focus on yourself.

EGO

> "People will love you
> People will hate you
> And none of it will have nothing to
> do with you"

Abraham Hicks

Ego

Imagine that you had everything you've always wanted in life. Good health, that lovely house with a nice car parked outside, beautiful holidays, a respectful and loving relationship, your family and friends around you, peace of mind... all of it. If you actually had everything that you wanted in life, would you still be upset that it's raining outside? Feel offended by your complaining colleague? Be jealous of your neighbor's new car? Do you really think that you would keep judging everything, including yourself?

All of this stems from the ego: the constant fear of not being enough, the perceived lack of knowledge and lack of control over everything. You let your ego take over to judge what's right and what's not. You keep pointing fingers towards everything and everyone, not realizing that the other three fingers are pointing towards YOU. If you see someone or something that bothers you, step away from the situation for a moment, look inside yourself, see why you feel that way and figure out where this feeling is actually coming from. Stop looking for the excuse that justifies your negative emotion.

So, instead of pointing fingers at the outside world, look in the mirror and start pointing those fingers towards yourself. It will take discipline and serious courage to really see yourself the way you are, to accept what you find and grow from there with more love and compassion towards yourself.

When you assimilate yourself with your ego, it will make you believe that you need to know and control everything and everyone around you. It convinces you to see everything from a perspective of fear and worry, in constant battle with yourself. But you can change that. Instead, think of a time when you felt truly happy, care-free, or loved. When you had real fun, and nothing else mattered. When you felt no urge to control everything. When you were actually *feeling* and not CONSTANTLY *thinking*. The real enjoyment of life comes from inside, from just feeling and not obsessively thinking.

In order to truly *feel*, you need to learn to be more present and to be more aware of your emotions and reactions, recognising their origin and what's causing them to take over you.

Experts estimate that our minds think between 60,000-80,000 thoughts a day! That's an average of 2,500-3,300 thoughts per hour, which is overwhelming to even consider. An average person is aware of between 5-10% of these thoughts, but all of these thoughts create your belief and control most of your life without you being aware of it.

The mind wasn't created to rule; it's more of a tool to translate this world, our emotions, to get us to where we need to be. But because our mind is bombarded from all directions by an information overload and doesn't have positive energy flowing to it as it should, it needs to protect itself. So it creates a shield. The ego.

Most of the things you think you need are in fact just the ego's insecurity or pride. The ego has a never-ending demand for things that will never satisfy it, complicating everything with terror and confusion. It creates a mask that we wear during our day-to-day lives, or a character that we enact out in the world, but more importantly, it takes over even in our own home, when we look in the mirror and forget that this is a façade.

The ego is not inherently bad. People say it should be banished to live a better, more loving life. They say that the ego drags you down, putting you in a cloudy state of blindness towards yourself and everything around you. This may well all be true, but you can never get rid of the ego – it's here to stay. And, actually, you need it to survive.

Your ego is a part of you. To get rid of it would be like sending away one of your children for being too naughty, too troublesome, too mischievous. Unless you plan to live in isolation, you have to accept that the ego is a part of you which you have to learn to work with, to get to know better, and to find new ways to communicate with. Only after doing this can you redirect the energy misspent by the ego in a positive direction, and nurture it with guidance and acceptance. You wouldn't leave your child alone in the kitchen surrounded by sharp knives and a lit gas stove. So why let your ego be in a harsh and dangerous environment, where it reacts out of panic and fear?

Because it has been unchecked and in control for so long, you start assimilating yourself with your ego and that's where the problem really lies. Instead of trying to lose or suppress a part of yourself, it's better to focus your attention on it from a neutral point of view, free from its influence, like an outside observer. This will help you study and monitor your ego so you can figure out its ways of control. This is the best way to understand and overcome it, and it is only possible when you look at your ego from a neutral, non-judgmental point of view. Without this neutrality, you'll only battle with yourself, and that's not the goal here.

One of the most powerful weapons the ego has is fear. Fear is just an illusion, a powerful illusion. This fear is not real, yet we have all fallen victim to it in one way or another. When I say fear is an illusion, I mean that if you have to enter a place guarded by a dangerous animal, or any other scenario that terrifies you, the fear that you may or may not be attacked is just an illusion. All the scenarios that you create in your mind about hypothetical situations are just illusions. The *danger* may be real, the unpredictable animal is there after all, but your fear in and of itself is an illusion that your mind creates, and this can have a tremendous impact on yourself.

To illustrate this point, let me tell you about Will Smith's skydiving experience, which I believe is a powerful lesson.

On a night out, after one too many drinks, Will agreed along with his friends to go skydiving the next day. When Will was by himself, he started panicking, imagining over and over again how he would jump out of the plane, and how all the possible disastrous outcomes might come to be.

He seriously questioned his impulsive decision. That is the moment that your mind is at its ''best''. Your mind creates the illusion of fear, playing out hypothetical horror movies in gruesome detail, trying to protect you from supposed danger. Your mind attempts to keep you under control, and in your comfort zone, where it thinks it's safe. That night, while he was in bed and couldn't sleep, Will hoped his friends were so drunk that they'd forget all about it the following morning. That was *not* what happened.

The next day, Will's friends showed up and were ready. He was terrified, as they all likely were. We are trained from a young age to hide these feelings of fear, as they show weakness, which affects how other people may judge or criticize us.

You don't want to come across as weak. Or, rather, your *ego* doesn't want to come across as weak. So, your ego whispers to you to put your mask on, pretend that everything is alright, act like you're still in control. But that couldn't be further from the truth. In reality, it's total chaos inside of you. Will was panicking so much that he couldn't sleep. His stomach was acting funny, but he didn't say anything about it. He didn't want to be the only one who wasn't going to do it. So, he arrived, underwent training, got on the plane and ascended to 14,000 feet.

In the plane, he saw the red, yellow and green lights, realizing that the green light would signal his time to jump.

Only as the door of the plane opened did he realize he'd never been at that height before with a door open and ready for him to leap through. After some of Will's friends had jumped, Will and his instructor got up and walked to the open door at the edge of the plane, "looking down on death", as he described it. This point is a critical moment - total panic can set in and your mind becomes highly alert. It imagines the worst possible scenarios, believing it's going to die, and by associating yourself with your mind, that thought can become a reality for you in a fraction of a second.

Will's instructor told him that they would jump on the count of three, but they actually jumped on the count of two, as people usually grab on at three. Despite the initial absolute terror that Will felt as they jumped, he realised a few seconds later that this was the most blissful moment of his life. He was flying. He also realized that it's at the point of maximum danger that he felt the minimum fear - "bliss", as he called it. That's what happens when your mind is out of options and finally lets go - in that moment, you just *are*!

The lesson for him was strong. Why was he so terrified the sleepless night before? Why was he panicking in the car on the way to the plane? We create these awful movies in our minds, combining the worst of the worst scenarios that may or may not actually happen. What's the real danger, and is it reason enough to sabotage our health and wellbeing in that way?

Fear is just an illusion, created by your mind because of its lack of control or knowledge. While Will lay in bed the night before, he felt the same emotions as he would have had he actually been on the plane. Until the moment you actually jump, there is no reason whatsoever to be scared. It just ruins your day, and ultimately your health, as your body can't understand the difference between what is real, and what is imagination. Whatever goes through your mind, becomes an experience for your body.

At the moment of the jump, Will should have been terrified, but it turned out to be the most blissful moment he'd ever experienced. He said something very powerful that I want to share with you: "God places the best things in life on the other side of terror, on the other side of maximum fear are all of the best things in life." To me, this is a beautiful thought.

When confronted with your fear, instead of running scared, embrace and overcome it. Turn that monster of fear into something that you can love and learn from. This is how you take control of your fears, rather than your fears taking control of you. Plus, you get to grow and be more confident in your day-to-day life and release some of that mud that you've been collecting. Don't be afraid to just let go and be yourself. *Feel* again, without judgment and fear. Stop looking towards anyone else's opinion or approval. Start approving yourself!

THE CHILD

> ❝
>
> *"The secret of genius is to carry the spirit of the child into old age, which mean never losing your enthusiasm."*
>
> **Aldous Huxley**

The Child

Can you remember what it was like to be a child? Can you remember the last time you were at a park and went on the spinning teacups, terrified by them but at the same time laughing, and waiting for your turn to go again? Can you remember playing games with your friends, and when it didn't go your way, instead of running back to your parents, you took a quick moment, thought creatively and came back with a new sure-fire strategy to win?

The problem with adults is that they lack this childish bounce-back. You face an obstacle, and take a break. But the question is, when is break-time over? Come back in the game with a better attitude, with a smile on your face, knowing that you've gained experience, that you've grown and that you're better prepared than last time. Find your enthusiasm and drive towards life. Stand up from that bench. Break-time is over!

You must be increasingly present and aware of the events surrounding you, but at the same time, you must be able to see life from a child's perspective. That's not to say you should embrace naivety or live with your head in the clouds, but rather you need to be more playful. You need to be aware of your own state, be more enthusiastic, shed stress and worry, and simply live in the moment.

Can you remember the last time you did something nice for yourself, and you were simply present in the moment, without worrying about money, work, or the plethora of things on your to-do list? When was the last time you actually absorbed the moment completely like you used to as a child? Were you bothered by whose vocabulary was better, what brands you were wearing, who had more money, and so on?

You didn't care about anything like that; you just enjoyed the moment. When was the last time you did something stupid with your friends? Do you still have people in your life that you can call friends, without conjuring negative thoughts?

I still remember sneaking out with two friends to a party fourteen kilometers away when I was sixteen. We caught the last bus, and the party began. It was amazing. We were having an incredible time. Until we found out that the first bus back was at six o'clock in the morning.

If I wanted to live another day, I needed to be in bed well before 6AM. My parents had no idea I was at this party, and as early risers, they would know that I snuck out in no time. I convinced my friends to start walking. I knew of another bus we could catch halfway, so off we went. We only had one jacket with us, and it was *freezing*, so each of us took turns wearing the jacket for five minutes at a time, on the dot! After walking an hour and laughing about how stupid yet hilarious our situation was, we decided to take a break to rest our legs on the side of the road. There was no traffic at that time of the night, so my friend with the jacket sat down, and my other friend and I sat around him just to keep warm. Feeling exhausted from the party and the long walk, we set our alarms for ten minutes and rested, only planning a quick recharge.

A man on a bicycle approached and, when he passed us, shouted: "What are you doing there?" and kept going. At that second, all three of us stood up and started shouting: "Hey stop, please stop!" We all realized the same thing: he had a bicycle and a jacket! But of course he wasn't going to stop for us. God, we laughed like crazy, not that we intended to take them from him, but more at the thought of it.

Still, the idea was that you could start seeing yourself and your situation from a different point of view when you're more relaxed and in the moment, and not caught up with the fear and details of everything you go through. When did we become so serious, always busy and on the run, never having time for ourselves or for the things we love?

Ask yourself this: at what point in your life did you decide to give up, or decide that you knew enough?

When did you decide to stop asking questions, to stop learning? And by that, I don't mean forcing yourself through yet another university degree just to *feel* like you're more educated. The word 'educated' comes from the Latin word 'educo', which means to bring up, to develop and grow from within. Education doesn't only come from lectures, essays and books.

Relax, take time for yourself and accept that you're not perfect - you never were and will never be, but that's *okay*. You're human. Because of your 'imperfections', you have got to experience so many things that made you the person you are today. There is not one perfect person on this earth.

The fact that we are not perfect is one of the best things about us - how else would we experience and learn if we were perfect? We would be in a state of total boredom. We would probably still be in a cave somewhere staring at a wall all day! But the fact that we are not gives us the drive to grow, to learn, to love, to go outside and experience life, to enjoy such a complex world and everything in it.

Take a good look back at some of your problems from the past. Did they not help you, make you grow, and turn you into the person that you are today? Understand the lessons you've learned and drop your baggage. Come into the present and stop looking for everyone's opinion or approval on how you are *supposed* to be and approve yourself instead!

Everyone is unique in their own way, which means that all of us have our own way of seeing things, our own reality, our own understanding of life and how it should or shouldn't be. How you think, the way you see things, and your beliefs dictate your reality, and if someone doesn't fit your standards, you start thinking that they are wrong and that you know better. But is there really a wrong way? How would you know? Compared to what? How do you know how another person has to be or what's best for them to do? How would you know their path in life and what kind of experiences they have to go through or not, to get to where they need to be?

Everyone has their own path in life. Stop sharing your opinions so much and focus on yourself. Study yourself and get to know yourself: your good, your bad, your reactions and where they're coming from. Make it a ritual. Because if you don't recognise and work on *your* perception of you, you'll end up accepting *other people's* perceptions of yourself and let this dictate your reality.

There is nobody in this world that knows you better than you, so instead of being guided by fear or other people's opinions, spend time working on yourself. Make this your main focus and really get to know yourself from a detached, non-judgmental perspective.

Study yourself and see why you do what you do. Discover your beliefs and where they come from. Are they yours, or are they adopted from those around you? Relax and take a deep breath - you can't keep driving without stopping for gas. Here's a great saying that has helped me: "Energy flows where attention goes." So, you must learn to be more present and in control of yourself, not lost at sea without a compass.

PRESENT

> " "Yesterday is history, tomorrow is mystery, today is a gift of God, which is why we call it the present"

Bill Keane

Present

Nothing else exists apart from the present moment. The past is gone, and the future is not here. The only time that matters, and that we actually have power over, is the present moment.

To achieve anything in this life, you have to learn how to be present. You can't keep building the future with your past - that will only lead to history repeating itself. Be grateful for the lessons that your past offers and learn to let it go. If you want a better future, invest your energy into the only thing that matters: the sweet, present moment.

There are many exercises that can help you be more present and aware, and I don't think there is a right or a wrong way to do it. They are all right for someone - just choose the one that works for you.

Here are some examples I have found to be effective:

During your day, as many times as you can, stop and pay attention to what is going on in your head, what you are feeling inside your body at that moment, and why. Do this from an outside, detached perspective. You will come to realise how much is going on inside of you without even being aware of it, and you'll recognise the thoughts and emotions that are controlling you and your life. If you want to take more control over your life and be more aware of your decisions and why you are making them, you need to take a break from everything and leave your mind alone to mute the chaos.

By constantly reminding yourself during the day to stop and be present, you will build yourself up to a point where you don't have to remind yourself to be present anymore - you just *are*. You'll be aware of what's going on inside, you'll start noticing why and how you think and find ways to improve or be more in control of yourself. Pay attention to your inner voice and who it actually is, and take better decisions for yourself. Don't forget that all of this comes with practice. Without daily practice, it won't stick.

We tend to neglect the small things because we think that they're not important, but when we do that, they gather together, and transform from something small to a huge elephant on our shoulders.

To understand this better, think of a time when you had to do something that required discipline, like sticking to an exercise routine or finishing that book, but you didn't do it because you kept telling yourself you'll do it tomorrow. Inevitably, the next day you will have kicked yourself a little for not having done it the previous day. As these little things are not priorities, it seems unimportant.

Still, if you keep up this habit of procrastinating, in time, you will start to judge yourself, criticize yourself and think of yourself as lazy and as a failure. As these little cracks accumulate, they build to a breaking point, leaving a desire to run away from everything, feeling overwhelmed and over-burdened.

This happens when you don't pay attention to the minor chatter, the little things that niggle at your mind. Pay attention to yourself, work on the small things and let the big picture pass for a while: take it one step at a time. Do that every day, and soon enough you will wake up, feeling lighter and ready to face the day.

Stop judging yourself and simplify your thoughts, because most of them are not even yours.

Another simple yet powerful thing you can do is to pick an object and stare at it for as long as you can in the present moment. I know how this sounds, but the first time you try, it won't take more than five seconds until your mind wanders.

You can't achieve anything if you are constantly thinking of a thousand things and can't focus your attention on a subject for more than a few seconds.

Pick an object. For me, I prefer a candle or a flower. Make sure you won't be interrupted, then sit down and look at it. Try to take in as much as you can from the color, the smell, the way it looks, the textures.

Be completely present in the moment and take in everything that you can: every color, smell, shape, all of it. And whenever you notice your mind wandering, bring it back.

Don't do this by trying to force your mind - that will just agitate it more. Instead, bring your attention back to the flower in the present moment, every time it wanders. Do that over and over again, like it is the first time you ever tried it, without judging or getting frustrated. You will be curious about how much you can absorb until you lose your focus again. You will find the game in it, and with enthusiasm and perseverance, you will achieve what you seek.

If you keep practicing this for a couple of weeks, you will notice a change inside of you. You will have more control of your attention, and you will be able to focus on the present with much more clarity. Those five seconds of uninterrupted focus will turn into fifty, which will boost your confidence. All of your attention will be used to actually focus on something of your choosing, with your energy being calm, aware and present.

Another way to help yourself is to start meditating. An easy way to do that is by making sure that you won't be disturbed and that you are not overly tired, as that can make you fall asleep.

Sit in a very comfortable position, close your eyes, and become an observer of your emotions and thoughts. Do not try to control or do anything in particular. Just notice from a neutral point of view whatever is going on.

After fifteen to twenty minutes, your mind will check on you to see if you are sleeping or not. The urge to move and to change your position will pop up very strongly. Ideas that you are in some pain or discomfort will be at the front of your mind. Now, remember that you are in a relaxed and comfortable position, and all of those feelings and thoughts are just your mind checking up on you to see if you are asleep or not. If you can ignore it, and if you don't move a muscle, your mind will go to sleep.

At that moment, a beautiful, light feeling will emerge in your body, and you won't be able to tell where your arms or legs begin and where they end anymore.

You will feel that you are more like a mass of energy that vibrates. You are whole. When you become whole, your five senses work at a low level, allowing you to feel your energy and control your emotions, to be present and memorize that feeling of oneness in the present moment.

When that happens, you go even deeper and you merge with yourself. Time doesn't exist anymore. You won't know if you are in that state for five minutes or fifty. When you get to that point, start focusing your attention on your chest area, on your heart, on the feeling of love emanating from you, and around you. It will be so awe-inspiring and powerful that you will likely smile uncontrollably. Do that enough times, until it becomes natural to be present, and in a good state.

Another exercise you can do to feel more present is to get up one day and leave your house without taking your phone with you. I know, the thought might be TERRIFYING at first. But don't worry. You'll be just fine. Doing this simple thing just once can show you how present you can be. Your mind might be under the impression that it will be scary or that you'll get bored without your phone, but I want to remind you that these are just wandering thoughts. To be truly present is more of a feeling, a state. You just *are*. And this is so fulfilling that it's impossible to get bored.

Another recommendation is to start taking increasing care of your physical body. It will help you to be more in control of your state and emotions. Work on your discipline not as a punishment, but more as an organized way of being.

There are many types of nutrition books or exercise programs. Pick one that works for you and your lifestyle and start working on yourself. Try not to judge or criticize yourself so much in the process as it will end up having the opposite effect and harming your body.

Masaru Emoto undertook many incredible studies of how much our thoughts and emotions influence water. One simple test he did, which you can do as well, is this. He took three glasses with rice and water. For a month, he said 'Thank you' every day to the first glass. To the second one, he spoke negative words such as 'You are an idiot', and he completely ignored the third glass. After 30 days, the first glass with rice started to ferment, releasing a pleasant scent. The rise in the second glass turned black, and the rise in the third one started to rot. Considering that the human body is around 70% water, you will definitely start changing the way you look and feel about yourself by changing how you talk to yourself. Your body can feel what you think about it and works according to your emotions.

A state of acceptance is also a state of being present. Being present and in a state of general acceptance helps you realize that life is not good or bad - it just *is*.

Try this: at the end of a wedding, or any event you want, ask the people coming out some questions. You will find that some of them had an amazing time, raving about how good the music was, and proclaiming they can't feel their legs from dancing so much, singing the praises of the food, while others will tell you that they couldn't wait to go home, and that they couldn't stand the music. You get the picture.

The point is that the wedding or event represents life, and it's not good or bad, it just *is*, and the way we choose to look at it determines whether or not we actually enjoy it.

In the words of Wayne Dyer: "If you change the way you look at things, the things you look at change." Make it all a game, stop compromising yourself and instead compromise the perception you hold of yourself. Look at it from a different perspective, from a different angle.

Try to remember an event in your past when you really wanted to get somewhere or get something. But, you saw no way of achieving that goal under the circumstances at that time, and there was nobody to guide you or bolster your confidence. Despite this, you just knew that you'd achieve your goal.

You had no idea how it would come about or even where to start. Still, you didn't let that pull you down or make you quit. All you knew was that you wanted it no matter what, and suddenly you got a phone call that put you on the right track, met someone or saw something that awakened an idea in you, and before you knew it, you'd achieved that thing without realizing how it all came about. I'm sure all of us have had at least one moment like that in our past. But the question is, how did it work, why did it work, and would you like to try it again?

THE LIST

> "
> "The first secret of getting what you
> want is knowing what you want"
>
> **Arthur D. Hlavaty**

The List

Once you manage to focus your attention on the present moment, take a pen and paper and write down exactly what it is that you want next. If you come up with more than one thing, rank these from highest to lowest priority. Really take your time, be present and be aware of what you decide to make your number one priority on the list, so that a day or a week later, you don't change your mind and lose focus, dividing your attention between different goals on the list. Take it one at a time. This is extremely important. If your attention is spread in multiple directions, you start to doubt your decision or lose your focus, and then you end up not achieving your specific goal. Focus on one goal, until it becomes natural to you, and stick to it!

As a suggestion, after you decide on your number one priority, make sure it is something you feel passionate about. You need to have passion and attraction towards what you *want*, rather than just what you think you need.

If you have no passion or enthusiasm, meeting your goal can become difficult and burdensome. After a while, you lose belief in your goal and question whether you're capable of meeting it. You become conflicted. You need to have the passion to be able to believe and to be open to receive.

For example, you may set making money as your number one priority, but in reality, this may not be the best goal to focus on.

This isn't because you don't want money itself, but because you're more passionate about other things that mean more to you. It's *those* things that should take number one priority on your list.

If you think about it, you want money so that you can acquire things, experiences, or have more time and freedom. So actually, your goal should be that experience, or that extra time that you want for yourself, instead of the money which is just a way to get there. Focus on what it is that you really want, take your time, be specific, and stick to it!

YOU AS A
TUNING FORK

> "Stop trying to change the world since it is only the mirror. Man's attempt to change the world by force is as fruitless as breaking a mirror in the hope of changing his face. Leave the world alone and change your conception of yourself."
>
> **Neville Goddard**

You as a Tuning Fork

"Your life is a reflection, you don't get what you want, you get what you are. You gotta be it to see it."

Steve Maraboli

There are a few laws that govern this world, and we're going to explore some of those now. One that you might have heard of is the law of attraction.

To understand how it works better, you have to know about the law behind it - the law of vibration. This states that everything is energy that constantly vibrates at a certain frequency. Nothing is at rest. Which means that, in relation to the law of attraction, like attracts like. You attract exactly the level of your vibration. This is reflected in your results in life, the way you live your life, everything that you have achieved, or failed to achieve, up until this point. You set your level of vibration, and what you attract will match this level exactly.

When you say that you try, but the law of attraction doesn't work for you, it's like saying that the law of gravity didn't work today. Have you come across any floating people? If the law of attraction 'doesn't work' for you, pay attention to your thoughts and your feelings, and see if they are actually aligned with what you want in the present moment. What state have you been in all day? What energy are you putting out into the world?

All you have to do now is imagine how it would feel if your number one goal actually became a reality. Focus on this feeling daily, and make it as strong and present as you can. Think about every possible detail regarding your goal to make it come alive.

See yourself in the future, the person you are when your goal, your dream, has come through, and ask yourself: How do I feel?

How does your answer to this question make you feel? How does life feel looking through those eyes?

Start creating scenarios and situations in your mind with people or places from your future self's point of view. The idea is to play with it until you get that feeling. Build an entire movie that gets you really feeling what it's like to have achieved your goal.

After a while, you will become more familiar with the movie and you will be able to simplify it into a single picture. By continuing to do the same thing, to feel yourself here and now exactly as in the picture, over time that picture will disappear, and all that will be left is the feeling and you present in it. You create a future by feeling in the present, not by being in the future that you are trying to create. Success is a feeling. As long as you still have a movie or a picture inside of you, you are in the future. But when all of that becomes just a feeling, you made it!

Then is the moment you start being creative and inventive. This is when you start seeing the doors that lead you to your goal. This is when coincidence and synchronicity appear. Don't lose your focus and put all your energy into one opportunity that you believe is the right one. When a door appears, you can get excited and you can get confused between the door leading to what you need, and the door leading to the thing that can get you to what you need. The important thing is to keep an open mind and not forget the main goal. Some doors are the answers, and some are just a way to the answer.

Now remember, you've done this before in your life. Don't get caught up in the details of how it will happen or in the worries that will distract you from that feeling. Everything in this universe is energy, and it all works on vibration. All that you have to do is match your vibration to the frequency of the feeling of your wish fulfilled, and the way will unfold.

Here is another practical example: take two identical tuning forks and place them on two wooden resonator boxes in the same room. Strike one of them. You will notice that the other one will start vibrating at the same frequency, in the same way, without even being touched.

Keeping this example in mind, if you really know what you want, how it feels, and focus your undivided attention in the present moment on already having achieved it, you will start to resonate with it. From that moment on, as I said, synchronicity begins, coincidences will start to happen, and opportunities will start crossing your path in ways you couldn't have even imagined.

I can't stress enough how important it is to focus your attention on your goal as if it has already been achieved. By doing that over and over again, you actually start to feel it on an emotional level and it starts to become natural for you to be in that state.

Sometimes, everything aligns so well that you don't have to do anything, and sometimes you are required to act on an idea or opportunity to make it happen.

Just keep an open mind when it comes to opportunities and always keep your vibration as if what you want is already reality.

You can also build the feeling of your goal in the present moment by taking a cold shower. Besides the fact that it increases your endorphins, improves metabolism, improves circulation, and improves your immune system, it also helps you get closer to your goal.

The moment that cold water hits your body, you are fully aware and present. At the moment when that happens, bring up the feeling of your goal already manifested. Do this enough times, and you will memorize the path to get there quicker, and know how it actually feels so you can do it at every moment of the day.

Another thing you can do, before you go to bed every night, is think back on your day, to the moment you awoke that morning. By doing this, you will notice that you can't really remember what you've done that day.

You know the main things you did, but that's it. You won't know how you felt or what you were thinking when driving to work, were busy with your kids or when you ate. In other words, the feelings and level of vibration that you put out into the world.

By reviewing your day every time you go to bed, you will be reminded during the next day to be more present, as you know that night is coming, and you won't remember much. Have fun with it - don't make it feel like a chore. Turn it into a game of creating energy levels. Enjoy it.

Remember that you can't go to the gym for a week and expect to have a perfect body. It takes around twenty-one days to form a new habit and a new way of thinking. So do it consistently every day and try to do it for more than twenty-one days. It may be hard at the beginning, but if you do it enough, it will become natural. You will have created a habit, without even realising that you are doing it.

Every single time you start something new, it will seem like a lot. Do you remember how stressful it was when you started a new job, or your driving lessons, and how the same thing felt after a month or so having developed the habit of doing it? Take it slow and be patient – take it one day at a time. If you want to be happy and have what you need, you have to start working on yourself, and do what you know you have to do. Stop waiting for someone or something to do it for you, to come and save you. That rarely happens. The good news is that you don't have to change everything about yourself. All you really have to change is the perception you hold of yourself, the way you vibrate.

In everyday life, you come into contact with all kinds of situations and problems that can make you doubt what you feel and cause you to lose your focus on finer details. Now, whenever that happens, think about this example:

Imagine that you've been wanting to watch a movie for a long time, but for some reason, you never got around to it.

One day, you visit a friend and on their TV is exactly the movie you wanted to watch, but you've caught it right at the end. All you manage to see is the happy ending (your goal). Although you saw the end of the movie, you're still curious to see the rest of it. So, you buy some popcorn, invite some friends over for a movie night, go home and get ready.

Your friends arrive, everything is set up, and you press play. The movie begins and the characters in it start getting into all kinds of problems. While everyone gets wrapped up in the plot and can't see how the characters will overcome their obstacles, you feel relaxed. You grab your popcorn and lay back. You know this is going to end well, so you can just enjoy the movie.

You know that all the troubles they are getting into are just a means to an end, or lessons they need to get to that happy ending. Now do the same in life!

When did it ever help you to stress or worry so much? It only clouds your vision, and if you know the end, if you really see and feel the end, you can enjoy the process. You can enjoy the movie and realize that the so-called "problems" are actually there to guide you back on your path, to help you grow so that you can reach that happy ending.

Once you get it, it's quite simple, if you don't like what you see in your life, take a step back and reflect on yourself, your state, your feelings and what you're sending out there. You are the cause, and the outside world is the effect. Stop trying to change the effect - it will never work. The only way to change it is to change the cause, which is YOU.

Think of a car as your thoughts or the direction that you are heading in. The fuel is your feelings, the thing that powers the car and gets it to where it is going more quickly. How fast the car gets to its destination all depends on the fuel, and if it stays on course or not, which YOU decide from behind the steering wheel. But, along the way, don't forget to enjoy the ride!

"Life is an echo. What you send out comes back. What you sow, you reap. What you give you get, what you see in others exists in you."
- Zig Ziglar

THE TRIGGER

> " "Life is really simple, but we insist on making it complicated."

Confucius

The Trigger

Most of the time, we live busy lives, and it's easy to get distracted and lose focus. To help you manage this better, you can create a personal trigger that will take you straight to that stage of bliss, of the wish already fulfilled, without going through the process again. To achieve this, you must focus your attention on your goal, make it as real as possible in the present moment, on an emotional level as we talked about earlier, and then link it with a trigger.

The trigger can be an object, a song, a picture on your phone, anything you have access to during the day. Just make sure that it's something personal that will remind you of your goal. So, every time you've done your practice and find yourself in that beautiful state of your wish fulfilled, listen, see or touch your trigger.

Do that enough times and after a while, it will work the other way as well, meaning that every single time you come into contact with your trigger, you will automatically go straight to that amazing feeling of your wish fulfilled, without doing anything else. In addition to that, this feeling is linked with peace and control, the state of the present moment and the positive emotions that you link with it.

You must do this constantly in order to form that connection between the trigger and that blissful feeling, which means practice, practice and practice. After that, you can relax, grab your popcorn, stay present and enjoy the movie. There is no fixed way to reach your goal. Stop limiting yourself to the ways you *think* you will get it - that rarely happens. Instead, keep your eyes open and get ready to be amazed.

REVIEW

> ❝
>
> "It had long since come to my attention that people of accomplishment rarely sat back and let things happen to them. They went out and happened to things."
>
> **Leonardo da Vinci**

Review

Perhaps this notion of seeing things from an energetic and vibrational point of view is new to you, but if you think about it, what do you have to lose if you give it a go? Apart from finally having a specific goal, it will put you in a good state mentally and physically throughout the day, allowing you to be more present and aware of your life. So, take a good look at yourself, learn to accept things for what they are and appreciate yourself for who you are. Remember that nobody is perfect and that's quite alright. Re-discover your enthusiasm, your drive, that kid inside of you. Really work on yourself to be more aware and more present in your life.

Learn to control your mind and take care of your body. Choose a goal and focus on it with gratitude, from the point of the present, being thankful for it already being here.

Feel gratitude towards it, and everything else in your life, as much as you can. A state of gratitude creates more states to be grateful for. Use the tools in this little book to maintain and grow that feeling throughout the day as much as you can. Every state or feeling you hold on to is like a seed that's growing inside yourself from which you'll harvest the fruit, so pay attention to what you are growing.

Considering the programs we grow up with, the way we were taught to be, and how this world actually works is madness... but madness can also be divine!

"Everything is energy and that is all there is to it.

Match the frequency of the reality you want, and you cannot help but get that reality.

This is not philosophy.

This is physics."

Albert Einstein

I sincerely hope that you've enjoyed this book.

Stay tuned!

Thank you!